# Copyright © 2023 par Jessica

ISBN : 9798387529399
First edition, 2023

## Transform Your Life with 1070 Daily Affirmations: A Guide to Positive Thinking

Welcome to "1070 Daily Affirmations: Transform Your Life with Positive Thinking," a book that is designed to inspire and motivate you to achieve your goals and live your best life. For over 20 years, I have been helping countless individuals transform their lives and reach their full potential. This book is the culmination of my decades of experience, knowledge, and wisdom, and it is my hope that it will be a valuable tool in your journey to personal growth and happiness.

Affirmations are a powerful tool that can help you transform your life. By repeating positive statements to yourself daily, you can overcome negative beliefs and attitudes that may be holding you back and replace them with empowering ones. In this book, you will find 1070 affirmations that cover a wide range of topics, from self-esteem and confidence to abundance and success.

Each affirmation is designed to be short, simple, and easy to remember, so you can incorporate them into your daily routine without taking up too much time or effort. By repeating these affirmations daily, you will begin to see positive changes in your life, such as increased self-confidence, improved relationships, and greater success in your personal and professional endeavors.

I believe that anyone can benefit from daily affirmations, regardless of their age, background, or life circumstances. Whether you are struggling with self-doubt, looking to improve your relationships, or seeking greater success in your career, these affirmations can help you overcome obstacles and achieve your goals. I encourage you to embrace this book as a daily companion on your journey to a happier, more fulfilling life.

#1 - « Great things are within my reach, and I am fully capable of achieving them»

#2 - « Change excites and motivates me»

#3 - « I approach attracting love into my life with an open and receptive mindset»

#4 - « Rather than dwelling on problems, I focus my energy on finding solutions»

#5 - « I thrive on challenging myself and pushing beyond my limits»

#6 - « Negative thoughts have no power over me; I refuse to let them drain my energy»

#7 - « I am blessed with abundance in all areas of my life»

#8 - « My loved ones appreciate and respect my gentle nature and kindness»

#9 - « Being present in each moment is important to me»

#10 - « I am the creator of my circumstances and manifest only what aligns with my desires»

#11 - « I wake up each day eager to start work, without the need for an alarm»

#12 - « Life is a constant journey of growth and learning, and I embrace every experience»

#13 - « My income potential is limitless; there is no ceiling to what I can achieve»

#14 - « Anything I set my mind to is easily attainable»

#15 - « My emotions vibrate at a high level, and I am not held back by anxiety»

#16 - « My amazing qualities have a positive impact on those around me»

#17 - « I am fortunate to have wonderful colleagues who are also great friends»

#18 - « I release attachment to outcomes, knowing that everything happens for a reason»

#19 - « Even when faced with opposition, I remain calm and composed»

#20 - « Seeking to understand others is a priority for me»

#21 - « I am energized and full of vitality»

#22 - « I focus on my own journey, releasing the need to compare myself to others»

#23 - « Each day, I intentionally create happiness and joy in my life»

#24 - « I trust in my ability to make wise decisions and choices»

#25 - « I harness my feminine energy to positively impact the world around me»

#26 - « Forgiveness is a natural part of my life, for myself and others»

#27 - « Abundance and goodness are my birthright, and I am deserving of them»

#28 - « Empowering thoughts always triumph over negative ones in my mind»

#29 - « My mind and body are strong and healthy, enabling me to achieve my goals»

#30 - « My work allows for inner transformation and personal growth»

#31 - « I am strong and capable of overcoming any obstacle»

#32 - « My life is filled with abundant success and achievement»

#33 - « I wholeheartedly believe in myself and my abilities»

#34 - « Others opinions have no impact on my reality; I choose my own path»

#35 - « I choose to see the best in others and seek out their positive qualities»

#36 - « Life is a gift, and I cherish every moment»

#37 - « Exercise is a way to show love and care for my body, rather than driven by insecurity»

#38 - « I learn and grow from my experiences with anxiety»

#39 - « Compassion and forgiveness are part of my daily self-care routine»

#40 - « I am worthy and deserving of all the good things life has to offer»

#41 - « Wisdom guides me in every decision I make»

#42 - « I love and accept myself unconditionally»

#43 - « Love, happiness, and success are my birthright, and I embrace them fully»

#44 - « I am recognized and respected as an expert in my field»

#45 - « My inner and outer beauty grows each day, fueled by self-love and care»

#46 - « My thoughts create my reality, and I choose to focus on my hearts desires»

#47 - « I am grateful and happy in my chosen profession»

#48 - « My relationship is a source of deep gratitude and appreciation in my life»

#49 - « I see myself as equal to all others, without the need to compare or compete»

#50 - « I trust in the universes divine plan for my life and am open»

#51 - «I reside in a state of contentment»

#52 - «I feel secure and at ease knowing that I spread love wherever I go»

#53 - «Confidence and relaxation come naturally to me in the workplace»

#54 - «Embrace positivity»

#55 - «I am wise and capable of learning from all situations and circumstances»

#56 - «My ability to lead an inspiring and uplifting life is within my reach»

#57 - «I have faith in my ability to tackle any challenges that come my way»

#58 - «My commissions increase each day»

#59 - «Being the top producer in the workplace is a constant achievement for me»

#60 - «I welcome men into my life who treat me as an equal, and I do the same»

#61 - «I am deserving of setting healthy boundaries for myself and others»

#62 - «I am proud of the person I am evolving into»

#63 - «I love and embrace my appearance daily, regardless of my body type»

#64 - «Helping others is a source of joy for me»

#65 - «I replace limiting beliefs with empowering thoughts»

#66 - «Forgiveness comes naturally to me»

#67 - «I feel deeply content with my life»

#68 - «I am deserving of rest and relaxation to rejuvenate my mind and body»

#69 - «I have complete confidence in everything that I sell»

#70 - «I am grateful for the blessings that manifest in my life»

#71 - «I am a gift to my loved ones and to myself»

#72 - «I interpret my emotions, and my reactions are not influenced by them»

#73 - «I appreciate the love that surrounds me»

#74 - «I relish in the feeling of personal growth in my daily life»

#75 - «I take other peoples opinions of me with a grain of salt»

#76 - «I am grateful for the love that exists both within and outside of me»

#77 - «Asking questions frequently helps me to be a better worker»

#78 - «Love and compassion define my essence»

#79 - «My day is consumed with positive habits»

#80 - «I love reshaping my body because it increases my self-esteem»

#81 - «I am a victor, not a victim»

#82 - «Adaptability is one of my strengths»

#83 - «I am deserving of all the goodness that life has to offer»

#84 - «I trust in my inner strength and resilience to overcome any obstacle»

#85 - «Personal growth is a constant pursuit for me»

#86 - «I enjoy my own company and find peace in solitude»

#87 - «I view stress as a signal that something is not right, and I can resolve it with ease»

#88 - «I will never give up»

#89 - «I am open to new financial opportunities and streams of income»

#90 - «Even when I dont feel great, I push myself because that is what winners do»

#91 - «I have faith in the power of positivity to attract more positivity into my life»

#92 - «Success is mine in every area of my life»

#93 - «Achieving balance in all aspects of my life is within my capabilities»

#94 - «I seek to understand others before offering my opinion»

#95 - «I choose to see the good in myself and others»

#96 - «With commitment, there is always a solution»

#97 - «Starting my day with positive affirmations sets the tone for a great day»

#98 - «I am unique and one of a kind»

#99 - «I am perfect just the way I am»

#100 - «At this moment, joy and contentment fill me up.»

#101 - «I appreciate all the experiences that have shaped me into the person I am today.»

#102 - «Miracles are expected to happen in my life.»

#103 - «I am surrounded by positivity and optimism, uplifting me.»

#104 - «This experience is teaching me how to control my emotions.»

#105 - «I deserve to reach my goals and live my best life.»

#106 - «Loving first is the key to being loved.»

#107 - «God hears my call for help and will guide me through.»

#108 - «Love is present in every aspect of my day.»

#109 - «My thoughts are only abundant and prosperous.»

#110 - «Prioritizing my own needs and self-care is an act of self-worth.»

#111 - «I am proud of myself and my accomplishments.»

#112 - «To my loved ones, I am the embodiment of love.»

#113 - «Love is my inherent birthright.»

#114 - «Overcoming challenges comes easily to me.»

#115 - «Seek help when necessary.»

#116 - «I trust in the power of positivity to manifest more of it in my life.»

#117 - «Choosing to eat healthily shows my strength and vitality.»

#118 - «I have a lot to offer to the world and will do so.»

#119 - «Today, I will focus on the present moment and appreciate it fully.»

#120 - «I maintain full focus and attention in class.»

#121 - «Living a life that aligns with my values and beliefs is within my capability.»

#122 - «I am continually aligning myself with my lifes purpose.»

#123 - «Persistence and dedication come naturally to me.»

#124 - «The infinite love of the universe is felt in my daily life.»

#125 - «Constructive criticism is a valuable tool for my growth.»

#126 - «I am surrounded by kindness and compassion from those around me.»

#127 - «I have positive and loving friends who uplift me.»

#128 - «Accepting that I am loved is freeing.»

#129 - «A community of like-minded individuals surrounds and supports me.»

#130 - «Passion and enthusiasm for life course through me.»

#131 - «I care deeply and affectionately, and the world acknowledges and values me for it.»

#132 - «Inner peace and serenity are within me.»

#133 - «I offer my care and affection wholeheartedly.»

#134 - «The value I bring is appreciated.»

#135 - «I have the power to leave uncomfortable situations.»

#136 - «Daily improvements come easily to me.»

#137 - «My imagination and creativity have tremendous power.»

#138 - «Everything I need for a happy and stress-free life is within me.»

#139 - «I am grateful for all the blessings in my life.»

#140 - «I am perfect in this moment.»

#141 - «I am a person of integrity and keep my word.»

#142 - «Great role models guide and teach me.»

#143 - «Love and understanding guide my interactions with my partner.»

#144 - «I am capable of creating a fulfilling and joyous life.»

#145 - «My friends see me as a leader and someone they can trust.»

#146 - «I am in a mutually loving relationship.»

#147 - «I love and accept myself deeply.»

#148 - «Meeting deadlines is effortless for me.»

#149 - «I am a loyal and supportive friend.»

#150 - «I embrace my uniqueness and love it.»

#151 - «I am a role model for my daughters to aspire to and for my sons to seek in a partner.»

#152 - «I hold a positive outlook on life.»

#153 - «I do not pass judgment on my anxiety or stress.»

#154 - «My memory is exceptional.»

#155 - «I am assertive while also respecting others opinions.»

#156 - «Courage and confidence are inherent to my nature.»

#157 - «I relish working alongside my fellow students as we strive for knowledge and personal growth.»

#158 - «I do not give anxiety the power or attention it demands, and it eventually dissipates.»

#159 - «I am fully capable of overcoming any emotion I encounter.»

#160 - «My colleagues acknowledge my value and demonstrate it in numerous ways within the workplace.»

#161 - «Despite my familys past, I am determined to change and succeed.»

#162 - «Achieving success is immensely gratifying.»

#163 - «My workplace fosters harmony and affection.»

#164 - «I understand that happiness is my innate nature, so I take pleasure in all aspects of my life.»

#165 - «Positivity and hope encompass me.»

#166 - «I embrace my flaws because no one is perfect.»

#167 - «I attract serenity and serene individuals into my life.»

#168 - «I embody all that is good in the world.»

#169 - «Each day presents a wonderful opportunity for me.»

#170 - «I possess the capability of achieving fulfillment and joy in my life.»

#171 - «Love is my primary choice of emotion.»

#172 - «I have confidence in my ability to attain my aspirations.»

#173 - «I am the architect of my own destiny.»

#174 - «My determination and perseverance enable me to accomplish anything I set my mind to.»

#175 - «I treat myself with kindness at all times.»

#176 - «I can make a positive impact on the world.»

#177 - «I deserve to pursue my passions and follow my heart.»

#178 - «The finest clients seek me out every day.»

#179 - «I only compete with myself to improve.»

#180 - «I exude tranquility.»

#181 - «My significant other and I share an equitable partnership.»

#182 - «I am stunningly attractive.»

#183 - «I am free of anxiety.»

#184 - «Caring for my body with sufficient rest and nourishment brings me joy.»

#185 - «I hold myself in high esteem.»

#186 - «This is an opportunity for me to enhance my thought processes and increase efficiency.»

#187 - «Punctuality is a top priority for me, and I always arrive on time to work and appointments.»

#188 - «I permit myself to be authentic and behave genuinely, without concerning myself with others opinions.»

#189 - «My referral base is continually growing because my clients feel valued throughout the entire transaction and beyond.»

#190 - «I do not need to change to be loved or attract love; I am perfect as I am.»

#191 - «Success is customary to me.»

#192 - «Opportunities for creative expression surround me.»

#193 - «I adore being a woman.»

#194 - «I always nourish my body with healthy food, demonstrating self-love.»

#195 - «Life is an ongoing classroom, and I am constantly learning and developing.»

#196 - «My self-esteem reflects my growth, and I am aware of this, committing to endless personal development.»

#197 - «I am worthy of admiration and appreciation.»

#198 - «Abundance is prevalent in all facets of my life, including money, romance, and love.»

#199 - «I am capable of adapting to change and embracing new opportunities as they arise.»

#200 - «I acknowledge that happiness stems from within, and I pursue joy and love within myself.»

#201 - «I am fortunate to have landed my dream job»

#202 - «With hard work and determination, I am confident in achieving my dreams»

#203 - «My scars are a testament to my inner strength and peaceful warrior nature»

#204 - «My heart swells with love for my country»

#205 - «My focus is on constant learning and growth towards my ideal self»

#206 - «I believe in myself and my potential knows no bounds»

#207 - «Both my body and mind are in a healthy state»

#208 - «I handle my fears with composure and effectiveness»

#209 - «I am capable of achieving balance and harmony in all aspects of my life»

#210 - «I am free to express myself and be true to who I am»

#211 - «I let go of the past and embrace the present with each passing day»

#212 - «Loving more brings me abundant gains with no loss»

#213 - «Every moment, my anxiety dissipates»

#214 - «Abundance fills all areas of my life»

#215 - «My family and spouse cherish and accept me for who I am»

#216 - «My self-confidence grows stronger with each passing day»

#217 - «I am accepting and embrace myself wholly each day»

#218 - «I am always open to receiving and giving love»

#219 - «I am worthy of love and deserving of it»

#220 - «If I do not believe in something I am offering, I will immediately stop and find something I do»

#221 - «My high self-confidence is a reflection of my self-love, not arrogance»

#222 - «I consciously monitor my thoughts, replacing negative ones with positive and empowering ones»

#223 - «I am grateful for the support and encouragement I receive from those around me»

#224 - «I cultivate long-lasting relationships and friendships with my colleagues»

#225 - «Prosperity comes effortlessly to me»

#226 - «Success was destined for me from birth»

#227 - «My loved ones appreciate and love me for who I am»

#228 - «I have or will marry my perfect match»

#229 - «My passion for life drives me towards success»

#230 - «Learning is exciting and enjoyable for me»

#231 - «My mind naturally gravitates towards positive thoughts»

#232 - «I am deserving of love and capable of giving it»

#233 - «I can achieve success in all areas of my life»

#234 - «Unexpected opportunities for growth and advancement come my way»

#235 - «My vision of success guides me through difficult times»

#236 - «Optimism and hope fill my being»

#237 - «My friendships help me create more success and love in my life»

#238 - «I learn from my mistakes and become a better person each day»

#239 - «I am capable of leading a life filled with purpose and meaning»

#240 - «Success in both my career and love life comes effortlessly to me»

#241 - «Love and romance are naturally attracted to me»

#242 - «My life is a journey towards fulfilling my destiny»

#243 - «I am grateful for all the blessings, no matter how big or small»

#244 - «I have a natural ability to get along with colleagues and customers»

#245 - «Living my passion and chasing my dreams allows me to create value»

#246 - «My being radiates unconditional love»

#247 - «I am surrounded by opportunities for growth and expansion at every turn»

#248 - «Others notice and recognize my natural success»

#249 - «Positivity and love are abundant in my surroundings»

#250 - «I have the potential to achieve great things.»

#251 - «I treat my mind and body with respect, ensuring their well-being.»

#252 - «When I feel a lack of love outside of myself, I turn inward and show love to myself.»

#253 - «I feel safe and secure in my true self.»

#254 - «The love and respect I receive from others is a reflection of my worthiness.»

#255 - «During times of stress, I focus on the positivity and good in life.»

#256 - «I persevere through any obstacles.»

#257 - «Being at the top of my class brings me joy.»

#258 - «As a resilient woman, I can adapt to any situation.»

#259 - «I accept and love myself, as well as others, for who we truly are.»

#260 - «I am enough, but I continuously strive to learn and grow.»

#261 - «I choose to replace the habit of worrying with the habit of loving.»

#262 - «My growth is supported and encouraged by the people around me.»

#263 - «I feel relaxed and at ease wherever I go.»

#264 - «Beauty and inspiration surround me in the world.»

#265 - «Feeling calm and positive brings me happiness.»

#266 - «Not having kids now does not mean I wont find the perfect partner and be a great mother in the future.»

#267 - «Self-discipline is a quality that positively impacts all areas of my life.»

#268 - «I love my life and am open to whatever it brings.»

#269 - «At the end of the day, I feel content with the work I have done.»

#270 - «Every experience, good or bad, helps me grow and helps others.»

#271 - «I feel protected and secure.»

#272 - «There are no limits to what I can achieve.»

#273 - «I have overcome challenges before and I can do it again.»

#274 - «Today, I choose to release worry and embrace peace.»

#275 - «I trust my own inner wisdom and guidance.»

#276 - «I surrender to a stress-free life.»

#277 - «Whenever negative thoughts about myself arise, I replace them with positive ones.»

#278 - «As the creator of my home, I feel empowered.»

#279 - «I am a nurturing presence to my loved ones.»

#280 - «As a fearless leader, I inspire others.»

#281 - «I am deeply in love with my life.»

#282 - «I find joy and entertainment in my work.»

#283 - «I am satisfied with my current job and am open to growth opportunities.»

#284 - «I move at the pace that feels perfect for me.»

#285 - «Opportunities for growth and self-improvement surround me.»

#286 - «I automatically let go of any negative habits or thoughts.»

#287 - «I am grateful for the small joys in my life.»

#288 - «My job is a manifestation of my career vision.»

#289 - «I feel a deep sense of love emanating from within me.»

#290 - «Peace and tranquility are present in all aspects of my life.»

#291 - «I choose to be polite and respectful towards others.»

#292 - «Even though I may have made mistakes, I am still a good person.»

#293 - «I am strong and resilient, able to withstand anything.»

#294 - «I accept and embrace both my good and bad qualities.»

#295 - «I embody love, am loved, and am lovable.»

#296 - «I truly see everyone as equal to myself.»

#297 - «I have complete trust in myself.»

#298 - «Abundance and prosperity surround me in all areas of my life.»

#299 - «Letting go is a powerful act, not a sign of weakness.»

#300 - «Encouraging others not only strengthens them, but also strengthens myself.»

#301 - «I am always grateful for my successes.»

#302 - «I am loved unconditionally for who I am.»

#303 - «I accomplish more and more in less time each day.»
#304 - «My potential and power are limitless.»

#305 - «I am highly organized.»

#306 - «I have the ability to live my best life.»

#307 - «I show love and compassion towards my friends.»

#308 - «I constantly feel the warmth of love filling my heart and soul.»

#309 - «Love is the most powerful tool in my arsenal.»

#310 - «I love the person I am evolving into.»

#311 - «I am successful now and will continue to experience even greater success in the future.»

#312 - «Positive energy and good vibrations are always surrounding me.»

#313 - «I have the power to transform myself and shed my old ways.»

#314 - «Love overflows within me and surrounds me always.»

#315 - «I am willing to do whatever it takes to excel in my field.»

#316 - «I live in a state of peace.»

#317 - «I allow my passion for work to motivate me and enjoy financial rewards because of it.»

#318 - «Gratitude fills me for the present moment.»

#319 - «Every situation and scenario in my life is leading me towards my desired position.»

#320 - «I trust my intuition to guide me towards what is right for me.»

#321 - «I have the strength to overcome anxiety.»

#322 - «My enthusiasm for work rubs off on my teammates.»

#323 - «I am an excellent listener.»

#324 - «I am worthy of taking time to rest and recharge.»

#325 - «I am grateful for the abundance in my life, both material and spiritual.»

#326 - «I am continuously learning and growing.»

#327 - «This does not align with my true identity.»
#328 - «I love and accept myself in the present moment.»

#329 - «Love flows to me in every moment of my existence.»

#330 - «Everything that happens in my life is divinely orchestrated.»

#331 - «I will recognize my soulmate instantly when we meet.»

#332 - «I inspire my friends and family.»

#333 - «Smile and breathe.»

#334 - «I am unique and special.»

#335 - «I attract love easily.»

#336 - «I may not be where I want to be, but I am actively working towards my goals both at work and in my personal life.»

#337 - «My creativity provides a perfect outlet for relaxation.»

#338 - «Love brings abundance into my life.»

#339 - «Today, I choose courage over fear.»

#340 - «I trust in the journey of life and all its lessons.»

#341 - «I am fully prepared to receive love in my life.»

#342 - «I am confident in my ability to succeed and get every promotion I desire.»

#343 - «I remain focused and undistracted by others.»

#344 - «I attract loving relationships by simply being myself.»

#345 - «I am surrounded by love and support from friends and family.»

#346 - «I will only settle for a career that truly aligns with my passions and values.»

#347 - «I will redirect my focus until this challenge passes.»

#348 - «I always stand up for myself and my values.»

#349 - «I am worthy of taking risks and exploring new opportunities.»

#350 - «My signing rate is always 100 percent.»

#351 - «I have faith that the universe will guide me towards my highest good.»

#352 - «Stress is guiding me towards my destiny and helping me let go of what no longer serves me.»

#353 - «My heart leads me down the path of freedom.»

#354 - «Love is present in all my memories and visions.»

#355 - «I possess the power to put a stop to this.»

#356 - «I am a courageous and wonderful person.»

#357 - «I can see the beauty in everyone.»

#358 - «I am grateful for every experience that has shaped me.»

#359 - «The world is full of beauty and wonder, and I am grateful for it all.»

#360 - «My flaws are unique and beautiful, and they make me who I am.»

#361 - «I am capable of achieving success on my own terms.»

#362 - «The world around me is filled with beauty and wonder, and I am surrounded by it.»

#363 - «Challenges bring me opportunities to grow stronger and more capable.»

#364 - «Only abundant beliefs operate within me.»

#365 - «I am capable of achieving anything I set my mind to.»

#366 - «I am deserving of confidence and power.»

#367 - «I deserve all the good things life has to offer.»

#368 - «I exude self-confidence.»

#369 - «I trust in my own strength and resilience.»

#370 - «As a woman, I enjoy expressing myself fully.»

#371 - «I have done my best, and that is enough.»

#372 - «I am a natural born winner.»

#373 - «I attract people who help me on my journey to unbreakable self-confidence.»

#374 - «I deserve to be wealthy.»

#375 - «I am open to love and it is seeking me out.»

#376 - «What I focus on, I attract, so I only focus on what I desire.»

#377 - «I prioritize the needs of others before my own.»

#378 - «I attract situations that empower me.»

#379 - «I only compete with myself and strive to be better than my past self every day.»

#380 - «I am worthy of having healthy and fulfilling relationships.»

#381 - «I only attract the best of everything into my life.»

#382 - «I believe in myself so strongly that nothing can shake me.»

#383 - «I choose to see the positive in every situation.»

#384 - «Positivity and optimism surround me in all aspects of my life.»

#385 - «I incorporate habits into my daily routine that reinforce my excellent self-esteem.»

#386 - «I love like a mother loves her child.»

#387 - «I am constantly making positive changes in my life.»

#388 - «My anxiety teaches me valuable lessons, and I am grateful for that.»

#389 - «Through self-development, my work self-image improves every day.»

#390 - «Success flows effortlessly into my life.»

#391 - «I am productive and skilled at multitasking.»

#392 - «My unique value is recognized and appreciated by my teachers.»

#393 - «I have the freedom to think and choose for myself.»

#394 - «I love and accept the size of my breasts.»

#395 - «Today, I release limiting beliefs and embrace infinite possibilities.»

#396 - «My vibration is filled with love.»

#397 - «I am open to receiving abundance from the universe.»

#398 - «I only allow love and positivity into my life.»
#399 - «I strive to please my customers and turn their frowns into smiles.»

#400 - «The love I offer is returned to me tenfold.»

#401 - «My default is to operate from a place of unconditional love.»

#402 - «By cultivating greater love within myself, I am drawing my soulmate towards me.»

#403 - «I respect and cherish my femininity.»

#404 - «All my relationships are loving and fulfilling.»

#405 - «I am grateful for my ability to both give and receive love.»

#406 - «I possess the capability to adapt to change and overcome obstacles.»

#407 - «My life is abundant, and I am filled with gratitude.»

#408 - «I am intelligent and skilled in creating success.»

#409 - «I am a beacon of light in this world.»

#410 - «Societys standards do not define me, nor do they dictate my appearance.»

#411 - «People know me for my capacity to love.»

#412 - «Climbing the corporate ladder is effortless for me.»

#413 - «I feel valued, included, and respected.»

#414 - «I am surrounded by loving and supportive relationships.»

#415 - «Today, I choose self-love and release self-judgment.»

#416 - «I am capable of finding solutions to any challenge.»

#417 - «My life is a testament to love.»

#418 - «Stress cannot restrain me; I am unstoppable.»

#419 - «I prioritize and cultivate self-love daily.»

#420 - «My vision of a perfect future is taking shape.»

#421 - «I am enough and doing my best every day.»

#422 - «I feel safe and loved in my partners embrace.»

#423 - «I am in control of my emotions, not the other way around.»

#424 - «Every setback only leads me to greater success.»

#425 - «I am the most hardworking person in the room.»

#426 - «Distractions do not deter me from my work.»

#427 - «I enjoy expanding my knowledge and learning new things.»

#428 - «I release negativity and inhale positivity and courage.»

#429 - «My love life is of utmost importance to me.»

#430 - «I can only change myself, not others or external circumstances.»

#431 - «Success and prosperity are within my reach, and I am worthy of them.»

#432 - «I prioritize efficiency and productivity in my life.»

#433 - «I am deserving of both self-forgiveness and forgiveness from others.»

#434 - «Each morning, I wake up refreshed and motivated to achieve my goals.»

#435 - «Love is my essence, and I am manifesting it in all aspects of my life.»

#436 - «What is the lesson I am meant to learn from this?»

#437 - «My work fills me with a sense of purpose and vitality.»

#438 - «I choose happiness every day.»

#439 - «I feel empowered by my continuous growth and improvement.»

#440 - «I am capable of enduring this challenge.»

#441 - «I have confidence in my unique path and purpose.»

#442 - «I am a model student, committed to learning and growth.»

#443 - «My peers respect and admire me.»

#444 - «I approach life with positivity and enthusiasm.»

#445 - «I am the master of my own destiny.»

#446 - «Though content with my current career, I remain open to new opportunities and my limitless potential.»

#447 - «I learn quickly and efficiently.»

#448 - «I possess all the tools I need to succeed and trust in my abilities.»

#449 - «I meditate daily on love and happiness.»

#450 - «The universe is conspiring to help me achieve my greatest success.»

#451 - «I am fully in control of every aspect of my life.»

#452 - «Despite the challenges, I am committed to persevering.»

#453 - «I strive to grow and improve every day to ensure my success.»

#454 - «I possess the ability to overcome any emotional obstacle.»

#455 - «I am guided by a strong sense of purpose and direction in my life.»

#456 - «Through ongoing personal development, I continuously enhance my value as an asset to my workplace.»

#457 - «I see myself as a trailblazer and a valuable contributor.»

#458 - «Inhaling calmness and exhaling anxiety and stress, I find peace.»

#459 - «I embrace my unique qualities and recognize my inherent worth.»

#460 - «My outstanding work ethic always matches my high standards.»

#461 - «I am ready to release any negative thoughts or emotions.»

#462 - «My past mistakes serve as valuable lessons to create a more abundant life.»

#463 - «I am receptive to all the opportunities and possibilities surrounding me.»

#464 - «I love with the same passion and excitement as if it were the first time.»

#465 - «Continual self-improvement boosts my self-confidence and sense of self-worth.»

#466 - «I refuse to entertain the negativity of others.»

#467 - «I feel exhilarated as my dreams materialize every day.»

#468 - «My love is pure and innocent, like that of a child.»

#469 - «I reap plentiful rewards, both physical and intrinsic, through my work.»

#470 - «I am actively pursuing my dreams with enthusiasm.»

#471 - «I experience a deep sense of tranquility and calmness.»

#472 - «My committed relationship is characterized by love and affection.»

#473 - «I approach test days with a relaxed and composed mindset.»

#474 - «My mind is sharp and focused, allowing me to excel at work.»

#475 - «Today, I choose self-compassion over self-criticism.»

#476 - «Every day, I take steps towards achieving success.»

#477 - «I am mentally and physically prepared to perform at my best every day.»

#478 - «I am secure and protected.»

#479 - «I embrace feeling out of place, knowing that it leads to growth.»

#480 - «Success means creating my own definition of what it is.»

#481 - «I prioritize punctuality in all aspects of my work.»

#482 - «Living this life makes me feel vibrant and healthy.»

#483 - «I am a strong, capable, and independent person.»

#484 - «I am free from self-doubt and self-limiting beliefs.»

#485 - «I always surpass my previous months achievements.»

#486 - «The opinions of others do not affect my sense of self-worth.»

#487 - «My belief in myself is unbreakable.»

#488 - «I understand the power of my mind and use it to create a successful life for myself.»

#489 - «My true beauty comes from within my heart.»

#490 - «Meeting new people brings me joy.»

#491 - «I appreciate and find wonder in the beauty of the world around me.»

#492 - «With hard work and self-belief, I am constantly improving my athletic abilities.»

#493 - «I find joy and satisfaction in both small and large tasks.»

#494 - «I surround myself with supportive and successful friends.»

#495 - «I visualize vivid colors to alleviate my stress and anxiety.»

#496 - «My creative ideas have the potential to be profitable.»

#497 - «I confidently express my opinions and ideas at work.»

#498 - «I am deserving of success and happiness.»

#499 - «I trust my intuition and inner guidance to make the best decisions for myself.»

#500 - «I bring a unique contribution to the world that cannot be replicated by anyone else.»

#501 - «I dont resonate with this emotion because it doesnt align with who I truly am.»

#502 - «I take pride in all of my accomplishments thus far.»

#503 - «I find enjoyment in both personal and financial growth through my career.»

#504 - «I possess all the necessary qualities and more to excel in my field.»

#505 - «I am grateful and at peace with where I am in life.»

#506 - «By facing my fears, I am empowered and build greater self-belief.»

#507 - «I imagine myself in a state of tranquility.»

#508 - «Life is an adventure, and I embrace it with enthusiasm.»

#509 - «Today, I choose to release self-doubt and embrace self-confidence.»

#510 - «I have the ability to succeed in all of my endeavors.»

#511 - «My soul radiates beauty and positivity.»

#512 - «I surrender all worries to a higher power.»

#513 - «I am skilled at finding solutions to problems.»

#514 - «I possess many unique talents and abilities.»

#515 - «I trust my intuition and decisions with unwavering confidence.»

#516 - «I hold deep respect for my parents and teachers.»

#517 - «I live in the present moment and savor all that it has to offer.»

#518 - «I appreciate success and attract more of it into my life.»

#519 - «I am self-sufficient and capable at work.»

#520 - «I have faith in my path and trust the journey.»

#521 - «Love comes naturally to me, and I find it wherever I go.»

#522 - «I am surrounded by a supportive and inspiring community.»

#523 - «I overcome challenges with ease and resilience.»

#524 - «I create both active and passive income streams with ease.»

#525 - «I look ahead with optimism and curiosity.»

#526 - «Learning comes easily to me.»

#527 - «I embrace getting older and celebrate each year of life.»

#528 - «I trust myself to make sound decisions and choices.»

#529 - «Everything will be okay, and I am strong enough to handle whatever comes my way.»

#530 - «Although I may not be where I want to be yet, I am making progress each day.»

#531 - «I have unwavering belief in my abilities, and others believe in me too.»

#532 - «I love and accept myself for who I am, not who I or others think I should be.»

#533 - «I am wonderful just the way I am.»

#534 - «Love is a fundamental part of who I am, and I express it in all forms.»

#535 - «I persevere through all challenges and come out stronger on the other side.»

#536 - «I am complete and whole, and I show compassion to myself every day.»

#537 - «When I feel stressed, I envision a calm and still lake.»

#538 - «I am excited and hopeful for what the future holds.»

#539 - «I am an entrepreneur who creates solutions out of peoples problems.»

#540 - «I have the power to create positive change in the world.»

#541 - «I am worthy of forgiveness and extend compassion to myself.»

#542 - «Every day, I become more calm, positive, and loving.»

#543 - «I gain confidence with each passing day.»

#544 - «Those around me believe in my success, and I do too.»

#545 - «I view failures as opportunities for growth and learning.»

#546 - «Despite stress attempting to overpower me, I remain in control of my emotions.»

#547 - «I am a highly valued employee.»

#548 - «Abundance and positivity surround me.»

#549 - «Every day, I am improving my ability to love.»

#550 - «I express gratitude for all the joyful moments in my life.»

#551 - «The universe takes care of me.»

#552 - «I love my partner and children without condition.»

#553 - «My soulmate and I are equally committed to finding each other.»

#554 - «Each new friend I make brings more love into our lives.»

#555 - «I love and accept myself as I am.»

#556 - «I believe in the transformative power of gratitude.»

#557 - «I avoid resisting anxiety because resistance only perpetuates it.»

#558 - «I trust that gratitude will bring more blessings into my life.»

#559 - «I deserve to receive unconditional love.»

#560 - «A sense of peace and calm permeates my life.»

#561 - «I have the ability to achieve anything my heart desires.»

#562 - «Today, I release past mistakes and embrace forgiveness.»

#563 - «I have faith in my own abilities.»

#564 - «I make my own decisions and form my own opinions.»

#565 - «I attract money with ease.»

#566 - «Love radiates from me wherever I go.»

#567 - «Love surrounds me always.»

#568 - «Confidence comes naturally to me.»

#569 - «I trust that the universe will provide everything I need.»

#570 - «Fear does not control me.»

#571 - «I am capable of more than I give myself credit for.»

#572 - «Cooperation is my natural state.»

#573 - «Each day is a blessing and an opportunity.»

#574 - «Visualizing myself with high self-esteem is my anchor for self-transformation.»

#575 - «My mind is powerful and can manifest my dreams.»

#576 - «I choose to view everything through a lens of love.»

#577 - «I seek happiness and love within myself so that I may manifest it outwardly.»

#578 - «I take things one step at a time, always moving forward.»

#579 - «When I feel unworthy, I meditate on my inherent self-worth.»

#580 - «I channel my anxiety into productive energy.»

#581 - «Gratitude fills my heart for the abundance of love around me.»

#582 - «My family respects me for the hard work I do at my job.»

#583 - «My relationships are lifelong and filled with love.»

#584 - «I always find myself in the best possible circumstances.»

#585 - «I enjoy pursuing my passions and hobbies.»

#586 - «Meditation helps me overcome stress and anxiety.»

#587 - «I am grateful for my past experiences, which have shaped me into who I am today.»

#588 - «I am grateful for all of my unique talents and abilities.»

#589 - «Time management comes naturally to me.»

#590 - «I am highly productive and efficient.»

#591 - «I am not defined by my relationship status.»

#592 - «Beauty and positivity surround me always.»

#593 - «My actions inspire and uplift others.»

#594 - «I have hope for a bright future.»

#595 - «At work, I consciously cultivate positive habits.»

#596 - «I am thankful for the numerous opportunities for personal and professional growth in my life.»

#597 - «I am unique and valuable.»

#598 - «I am optimistic about the future.»

#599 - «My surroundings provide ample chances for me to learn and develop.»

#600 - «I deserve to pursue my passions and aspirations.»

#601 - «I feel at ease and content in the present moment.»

#602 - «Continuously improving myself is a top priority.»

#603 - «I am open and receptive to coaching and guidance in my workplace.»

#604 - «I have the ability to spread love consistently.»

#605 - «I choose to define myself based on my own perception, rather than the opinions of others.»

#606 - «I rise above any drama that may occur.»

#607 - «I appreciate and recognize beauty in places where others may not.»

#608 - «I am productive and effective.»

#609 - «I believe in myself and my capabilities to achieve success.»

#610 - «I take pride in the daily actions I take in my work.»

#611 - «I practice self-love and care on a daily basis.»

#612 - «My passion and drive inspire others.»

#613 - «Bad days do not detract from my good days.»

#614 «I excel at taking tests.»

#615 - «I possess the innate ability to give and receive endless love.»

#616 - «When faced with stress, I am grateful for the positive aspects of my life.»

#617 - «My life has meaning, and I see this purpose reflected everywhere I go.»

#618 - «I adopt a mindset of abundance and prosperity.»

#619 - «Today, I choose positivity over negativity.»

#620 - «Worrying will not change my circumstances, so I choose to replace worry with hope.»

#621 - «I only communicate loving thoughts to my partner.»

#622 - «I am open to experiencing a higher level of love than I previously thought possible.»

#623 - «I am in control of my emotions, and they do not control me.»

#624 - «I strive to improve myself daily, because I love and respect myself.»

#625 - «I bring positivity and light to my workplace.»

#626 - «I trust my resilience and ability to overcome challenges.»

#627 - «I persist in my pursuits.»

#628 - «I see the best in myself and others.»

#629 - «I am surrounded by positivity and optimism.»

#630 - «I comprehend my schoolwork and take pleasure in completing it.»

#631 - «I have an open mind to all the potential opportunities in my life.»

#632 - «My potential is limitless.»

#633 - «Romance brings joy and fulfillment to my life.»

#634 - «I derive satisfaction from inspiring other women.»

#635 - «I have all the financial resources I need.»

#636 - «I possess exceptional writing skills.»

#637 - «Speak up and express yourself.»

#638 - «I am confident in my unique strengths and talents.»

#639 - «I use exercise as a healthy outlet for stress.»

#640 - «I have the strength to overcome challenges and move forward.»

#641 - «I am deserving of a life that brings me happiness and fulfillment.»

#642 - «I am confident in my skills and abilities.»

#643 - «My family loves and supports me unconditionally.»

#644 - «I release any limiting beliefs that hold me back.»

#645 - «I have a unique and valuable contribution to offer the world.»

#646 - «While I find happiness in my career, I know that it can be found in many other aspects of my life.»

#647 - «I enjoy meeting new people and socializing.»

#648 - «I trust in my ability to conquer any challenge that arises.»

#649 - «I am fully present and engaged in both my classes and my life.»

#650 - «My mind is open to abundance and all new opportunities.»

#651 - «My motivation is always at its peak.»

#652 - «I am a beacon of optimism, radiating positivity wherever I go.»

#653 - «My life is filled with endless streams of peace and happiness.»

#654 - «My habits cultivate self-discipline, which in turn inspires confidence in myself.»

#655 - «Through the power of my thoughts and beliefs, I am able to create my own reality.»

#656 - «I show those around me how much I care for them.»

#657 - «My dreams and aspirations have no boundaries.»

#658 - «My marriage is a never-ending source of love and affection.»

#659 - «Everyone seeks love, and I am capable of providing it.»

#660 - «I am free to pursue my passions and be well-compensated for them.»

#661 - «I cherish the vibrancy and energy of youth and will maintain it throughout my life.»

#662 - «I remain optimistic and keep looking forward, even during times of stress.»

#663 - «I trust in my intuition and inner wisdom to guide me in all aspects of my life.»

#664 - «My unshakeable belief in myself and my abilities paves the way for my success.»

#665 - «I have limitless potential.»

#666 - «I deserve all the love, happiness, and success that life has to offer.»

#667 - «I view everything in life as an exciting adventure.»

#668 - «My gender does not define who I am.»

#669 - «I am desirable simply for being myself.»

#670 - «I am a natural leader.»

#671 - «I move through life with the knowledge that I am loved and supported.»

#672 - «My love and compassion have the power to heal wounds.»

#673 - «I listen to my body and give it what it needs.»

#674 - «I am confident in my sexuality and embrace it fully.»

#675 - «I expect great things to come to me in unexpected ways.»

#676 - «I am always open and eager to learn new things.»

#677 - «I trust my heart and follow its guidance.»

#678 - «Feeling lost is an opportunity to find the best path forward.»

#679 - «I love myself completely and allow others to love me in return.»

#680 - «Success flows effortlessly in all aspects of my life.»

#681 - «I embrace motherhood and feel fulfilled in my role as a mother.»

#682 - «I am grateful for the lessons that life has taught me.»

#683 - «This moment is temporary, and I will emerge stronger for having experienced it.»

#684 - «I radiate calmness and confidence in everything I do.»

#685 - «My unique talents and strengths make me an indispensable asset in the workplace.»

#686 - «I use my gifts to bring joy and fulfillment to myself and others.»

#687 - «It is safe and healthy to express my emotions and goals.»

#688 - «My life is filled with abundance in all forms.»

#689 - «I appreciate and cherish the simple pleasures in my life.»

#690 - «I am prosperous and abundant in all aspects of my life.»

#691 - «I love myself deeply, knowing that true happiness comes from within.»

#692 - «I am the creator of my own destiny.»

#693 - «Everything in my world is exactly as it should be.»

#694 - «I welcome and accept change as an integral part of life.»

#695 - «When anger arises, compassion flows through me.»

#696 - «Each day presents new opportunities to look forward to.»

#697 - «My intuition serves as a reliable guide in my daily life.»

#698 - «Colleagues seek out my expertise and knowledge.»

#699 - «I am easy to get along with and enjoy positive relationships.»

#700 - «My aspirations reach for the stars.»

#701 - «I possess inner beauty and radiate it outwardly.»

#702 - «Trusting in the universes plan for me brings peace and comfort.»

#703 - «I view cold calls as warm opportunities.»

#704 - «I see failure as a chance to learn and grow.»

#705 - «I confidently overcome any challenge that comes my way.»

#706 - «Being a mother, sister, and aunt brings immense joy and fulfillment.»

#707 - «My athleticism contributes to my overall well-being.»

#708 - «I gracefully age and gain wisdom with each passing year.»

#709 - «My effective study habits lead to academic success.»

#710 - «I acknowledge my positive qualities and use my flaws as opportunities for self-improvement.»

#711 - «I possess extensive knowledge and expertise in the products and services I offer.»

#712 - «I strive for self-mastery in the workplace.»

#713 - «I am a joyful child of God.»

#714 - «I embrace positivity and optimism, leaving negativity behind.»

#715 - «I find solutions to my problems with ease.»

#716 - «Abundance and success are drawn to me.»

#717 - «I am a quick and efficient learner.»

#718 - «I trust that God has a perfect plan for my life and follow His path with confidence.»

#719 - «I am abundance and prosperity in all aspects of my life.»

#720 - «I maintain a positive outlook and do not worry about what others fret over.»

#721 - «My life is filled with supportive and loving relationships.»

#722 - «Positive thinking empowers me to manifest my desires.»

#723 - «I am surrounded by kind and loving individuals.»

#724 - «I believe that anything is possible with hard work and determination.»

#725 - «I am deserving of love and appreciation from those around me.»

#726 - «I release stress from my body with ease.»

#727 - «Kindness is a natural part of who I am.»

#728 - «My life has a meaningful purpose.»

#729 - «I attract only healthy and loving relationships into my life.»

#730 - «I am deserving of admiration and respect.»

#731 - «I contribute to making the world a better place.»

#732 - «My innovative ideas and collaborations lead to success.»

#733 - «I am grateful for the abundance and blessings in my life.»

#734 - «I trust in my unique perspective and the power of my voice.»

#735 - «Today, I choose to release limiting beliefs and embrace my full potential.»

#736 - «Love is the most powerful force in the universe.»

#737 - «I am grateful for my unique gifts and talents.»

#738 - «I treat myself and others with kindness and respect.»

#739 - «My creator loves me unconditionally.»

#740 - «I trust in my ability to make wise decisions.»

#741 - «Success comes naturally to me.»

#742 - «I release myself from the pain caused by others and embrace my freedom.»

#743 - «No matter what, I always keep my word.»

#744 - «I possess the ability to achieve both success and fulfillment in my life.»

#745 - «My creativity knows no bounds.»

#746 - «I have faith in the process of growth and transformation.»

#747 - «I express gratitude for every opportunity that comes my way.»

#748 - «My own strength and resilience are a source of trust for me.»

#749 - «The master of my life is me.»

#750 - «I take pleasure in holding high self-worth and ideals.»

#751 - «The thought of succeeding in all areas of my life fills me with excitement.»

#752 - «Before I speak, I choose to love.»

#753 - «Success is at the core of who I am.»

#754 - «Life has taught me many lessons, and for all of them, I am grateful.»

#755 - «I am fearless in the face of adversity.»

#756 - «I possess all the necessary attributes to achieve success.»

#757 - «I remain prepared, so I dont need to get prepared.»

#758 - «I trust the process to guide my path.»

#759 - «My life is continually evolving and progressing.»

#760 - «Daily, I present myself at my best, which strengthens my self-confidence.»

#761 - «Anything I envision can become a reality.»

#762 - «I keep my work and family lives separate.»

#763 - «You are incredibly capable.»

#764 - «I am more significant than my stress.»

#765 - «I am a fantastic person.»

#766 - «I work hard to achieve my goals.»

#767 - «I attract self-confident friends who contribute to my growth.»

#768 - «Working under pressure is easy for me.»

#769 - «I am always surrounded by beauty and positivity.»

#770 - «I am deserving of unconditional love and attract it into my life.»

#771 - «I am receptive to all forms of wealth outside of my primary job.»

#772 - «My life is overflowing with abundance and prosperity, which I am grateful for.»

#773 - «Every aspect of my life is beautiful, and I am thankful for it.»

#774 - «My life is full of loving and supportive individuals.»

#775 - «I am calm and composed.»

#776 - «I recognize that growth is necessary to become more.»

#777 - «I am worthy of taking care of my physical, mental, and emotional well-being.»

#778 - «At work, I feel like a winner.»

#779 - «I am capable of achieving my goals and aspirations.»

#780 - «Today, I choose to let go of self-doubt and embrace confidence.»

#781 - «I provide support and encouragement to my family.»

#782 - «I trust in my resilience and ability to recover from setbacks.»

#783 - «I am deserving of taking up space and expressing myself authentically.»

#784 - «I have more control over my life than I ever thought possible.»

#785 - «Today, I choose to let go of judgment and embrace compassion.»

#786 - «I consistently close the highest number of sales each month.»

#787 - «Losing weight brings me joy because it promotes self-love and overall well-being.»

#788 - «I actively pursue and cultivate peace in all my relationships.»

#789 - «I possess the ability to create my own happiness.»

#790 - «Living in the present moment and releasing the past is within my capabilities.»

#791 - «I am determined and diligent in the pursuit of my goals.»

#792 - «I have the power to effect change in myself.»

#793 - «I embrace my completeness and wholeness as I am.»

#794 - «Abundance and prosperity flow into my life because I am worthy.»

#795 - «I embody the strength of a warrior.»

#796 - «Love and joy fill me in this present moment.»

#797 - «I excel at work with exceptional efficiency.»

#798 - «I take pride in my expertise at work.»

#799 - «I forgive those I once condemned, and do so with love.»

#800 - «My identity is not defined by my genetics or family history.»

#801 - «Abundance surrounds me in every aspect of my life.»

#802 - «I welcome growth and development in all areas of my life.»

#803 - «Love follows me wherever I may go.»

#804 - «My focus is solely on love and beauty.»

#805 - «I possess the capability to conquer any fear or doubt.»

#806 - «Opportunities for creativity and self-expression surround me.»

#807 - «I navigate stress with love and positivity.»

#808 - «Here and now, I am safe and secure.»

#809 - «I am a masterful and successful salesperson, attracting clients effortlessly.»

#810 - «Those around me uplift and support me, empowering me to achieve my dreams.»

#811 - «I have a clear plan for my lifes journey.»

#812 - «The confidence of high self-esteem fills me with love.»

#813 - «Gratitude fills me for the small moments of joy and happiness in my life.»

#814 - «Joy and happiness are abundant in my life, present in all opportunities.»

#815 - «I am my own confidant, a true and supportive friend to myself.»

#816 - «Every challenge I face makes me stronger and better.»

#817 - «The work I do brings valuable benefits to society.»

#818 - «My innate nature is one of success and abundance.»

#819 - «I treat myself and others with kindness and compassion.»

#820 - «I pursue knowledge on my own terms, recognizing its true power.»

#821 - «My relationships with my teachers are healthy and beneficial.»

#822 - «Happiness and joy are rightfully mine to experience.»

#823 - «My intuition is a trustworthy guide.»

#824 - «Today, I release judgment and embrace acceptance.»

#825 - «I have a unique purpose for being here.»

#826 - «I am thankful for every opportunity to learn and grow in life.»

#827 - «I excel at my craft and feel confident in my abilities.»

#828 - «I have deep love and appreciation for myself.»

#829 - «My clients view me as an expert in my field.»

#830 - «Abundant opportunities for growth and learning surround me.»

#831 - «I am pure love and compassion, beyond my passing thoughts and feelings.»

#832 - «I effortlessly deflect negative thoughts and energy.»

#833 - «I embody honesty and truthfulness.»

#834 - «I feel valued and respected in my work environment.»

#835 - «Its okay to move on from this job, and I have the courage to do so.»

#836 - «I recognize stress as a signal to look deeper for underlying causes, and I let it pass.»

#837 - «Its normal to feel difficult emotions, but I channel them into productive pursuits.»

#838 - «My unwavering belief in myself allows me to manifest my dreams into reality.»

#839 - «I see the greatness in every person I encounter.»

#840 - «Each appointment I attend is flawless, and I enjoy connecting with my clients.»

#841 - «Joy and laughter surround me always.»

#842 - «My divine destiny unfolds perfectly each day.»

#843 - «I am peaceful and optimistic.»

#844 - «My inner wisdom and intuition guide me towards my highest good.»

#845 - «I am deserving of love and acceptance.»

#846 - «I attract success effortlessly.»

#847 - «I manifest all that is aligned with my souls desires.»

#848 - «I look forward to each workday with growing excitement.»

#849 - «I am worthy of love and respect exactly as I am.»

#850 - «I keep my word and earn the respect of those around me.»

#851 - «My mind is creative and powerful beyond measure.»

#852 - «I trust my innate ability to manifest my deepest desires and dreams.»

#853 - «Gratitude fills me for simply being myself.»

#854 - «I am a powerful, confident woman.»

#855 - «Every challenge Ive faced has led to growth and evolution, and I am grateful for them.»

#856 - «The perfect partner is entering my life at the right time.»

#857 - «I approach awkward situations with humor and grace.»

#858 - «My heart is open and receptive to love and connection.»

#859 - «I am ready and willing to receive abundance and success.»

#860 - «Today, I fully embrace the present moment and let go of the past.»

#861 - «These positive affirmations uplift and inspire me as an adult.»

#862 - «My family holds me in high regard and respects me.»

#863 - «I have a serious side but can still find humor in unexpected moments.»

#864 - «I cherish being with my soul mate and embrace the growth of our love each day.»

#865 - «I deserve to be loved and respected.»

#866 - «Everything is unfolding perfectly and I trust in the universes plan.»

#867 - «I embody pure, unconditional love.»

#868 - «I attract people who genuinely want to love and support me.»

#869 - «I am constantly at peace within myself and with the world around me.»

#870 - «I am a unique and beautiful creation.»

#871 - «I manage my time effectively, like a successful person would.»

#872 - «Genuine love and romance are drawn to me.»

#873 - «My goals come to fruition with ease.»

#874 - «My work environment inspires and motivates me.»

#875 - «I trust in my ability to make wise and confident decisions.»

#876 - «I wake up each day feeling energized and passionate about life.»

#877 - «I can overcome any challenge by taking a deep breath and starting anew.»

#878 - «I excel as a student and continue to learn and grow.»

#879 - «I am deserving of all good things in life.»

#880 - «I trust my inner wisdom and intuition to guide me in the right direction.»

#881 - «My colleagues and boss recognize my productivity and contributions to the workplace.»

#882 - «My positive and optimistic attitude attracts supportive and helpful people.»

#883 - «My success allows me to make a significant impact in bettering humanity.»

#884 - «I use self-discipline to achieve my goals efficiently and effectively.»

#885 - «I am not afraid to love deeply and fully.»

#886 - «I am intelligent, witty, and humorous.»

#887 - «I will excel in my chosen career and become a great success.»

#888 - «If my current career path doesnt resonate with my heart, I have the courage to make a change.»

#889 - «I am grateful for the love and support in my life.»

#890 - «I am able to express my emotions with clarity and honesty.»

#891 - «I have confidence in my unique talents and abilities.»

#892 - «I am a goddess who lives a fulfilling and joyful life.»

#893 - «I lead with love and courage in all aspects of my life.»

#894 - «I am confident in my physical appearance and own my beauty.»

#895 - «Overcoming fear comes naturally to me.»

#896 - «I possess unlimited mental focus and concentration on my tasks.»

#897 - «I choose to love and forgive my enemies, bringing me inner peace.»

#898 - «Listening is just as important as speaking in effective communication.»

#899 - «I persevere until I achieve success.»

#900 - «I work hard to advance in my career.»

#901 - «I have unwavering faith in myself and my abilities.»

#902 - «I embrace and love my unique physical appearance, knowing I was created perfectly.»

#903 - «I pursue my dreams with relentless determination, regardless of naysayers.»

#904 - «I am optimistic and courageous in facing lifes challenges.»

#905 - «I am worthy of dedicating time to my passions and interests.»

#906 - «My mind is powerful and capable of manifesting my desires.»

#907 - «I have faith in the universe and trust that good things will come to me.»

#908 - «I adapt easily and effortlessly to change.»

#909 - «I choose to expend my energy in love instead of hate.»

#910 - «I have complete belief and confidence in myself.»

#911 - «The more love I give, the more love I receive.»

#912 - «I am dependable and honest in my workplace.»

#913 - «I confidently express my thoughts and opinions.»

#914 - «Like water, I flow through negative situations with ease and resilience.»

#915 - «Being present during my female cycles brings me joy.»

#916 - «I have complete faith in my abilities and skills.»

#917 - «I am driven and decisive in all aspects of my life.»

#918 - «Success comes to me with ease.»

#919 - «I refuse to place limits on myself in the workplace.»

#920 - «I am worthy of all the blessings that come my way.»

#921 - «I make a conscious effort to live up to my full potential every day.»

#922 - «Both my family and the public recognize my success.»

#923 - «No obstacle can stand in the way of my determination.»

#924 - «Artistry is a natural part of who I am.»

#925 - «My intuition is a valuable tool that guides me towards success.»

#926 - «Love beyond comprehension surrounds me.»

#927 - «My feminine power is a source of strength.»

#928 - «I feel confident and comfortable in my own skin.»

#929 - «I go above and beyond at work and am rewarded accordingly.»

#930 - «My mind is peaceful and calm.»

#931 - «I accept myself for who I am, regardless of what others may think.»

#932 - «Unexpected sources of wealth flow towards me.»

#933 - «I deserve to live a life full of purpose and meaning.»

#934 - «The power to create the life I desire lies within me.»

#935 - «Love and compassion are the only things that truly define me.»

#936 - «I deserve love and respect from others.»

#937 - «A raise and promotion are in my near future.»

#938 - «I find power and joy from within myself.»

#939 - «Everywhere I look, I see prosperity.»

#940 - «I release tension in my shoulders, jaw, and neck.»

#941 - «I am at peace with the current state of my life.»

#942 - «Inner peace and contentment are achievable for me.»

#943 - «Positive and loving relationships come easily to me.»

#944 - «My smile radiates warm, motherly love.»

#945 - «I am grateful for the abundance of love and support in my life.»

#946 - «Healthy eating habits bring me pleasure.»

#947 - «I can become a successful leader with hard work and dedication.»

#948 - «I am incredibly beautiful both inside and out.»

#949 - «I embrace change and am excited about the person I am becoming.»

#950 - «I have control over my emotions.»

#951 - «I am filled with courage and bravery to face any challenge.»

#952 - «I trust in the universe to guide me towards my highest good.»

#953 - «I am worthy of love and happiness in all areas of my life.»

#954 - «Love, success, and kindness flow easily and naturally towards me.»

#955 - «I possess infinite potential for success.»

#956 - «Every experience is an opportunity for growth and learning.»

#957 - «I am grateful for my unique gifts and talents that lead me towards success.»

#958 - «I possess limitless talents and abilities that benefit others.»

#959 - «I am attracting the perfect mate that aligns with my hearts desires.»

#960 - «I am a wonderful friend to myself.»

#961 - «I am at the perfect age to experience all that life has to offer.»

#962 - «I have the ability to create a life that aligns with my values and beliefs.»

#963 - «I learn from my mistakes and continue to grow into a strong, empowered woman.»

#964 - «The experiences that have shaped me into the person I am today are all reasons for me to feel grateful.»

#965 - «As a woman who embraces her flaws, I inspire others who are struggling to do the same.»

#966 - «I am open to change and willing to let go of anything that no longer serves me.»

#967 - «I am in control of my destiny and steer my life with a firm hand.»

#968 - «The passionate and creative individuals surrounding me are a source of great love and inspiration.»

#969 - «I am young and revel in my youthful spirit.»

#970 - «My anxiety gradually diminishes in size until it fades away completely.»

#971 - «My love extends beyond my physical being to the very depths of my soul.»

#972 - «I am a woman who embodies depth and purpose.»

#973 - «I love and cherish my body, always and forever.»

#974 - «Every event in my life is meaningful and happens for a reason.»

#975 - «I release stress, knowing that it is merely a temporary energy passing through me.»

#976 - «I am capable of overcoming any obstacle or setback that comes my way.»

#977 - «I embrace myself wholeheartedly, without any reservations or conditions.»

#978 - «I envision my meetings unfolding seamlessly, and that is precisely what happens.»

#979 - «I am always surrounded by the love and support of those closest to me.»

#980 - «I adore trying new activities and exploring fresh ideas.»

#981 - «I find equilibrium between work and rest, creating a balanced life.»

#982 - «I take full responsibility for my work, both the good and the bad.»

#983 - «I recognize the new income opportunities that present themselves to me.»

#984 - «I trust that self-love has the power to bring about transformative change in my life.»

#985 - «A peaceful existence is my true destiny, and I am certain of this.»

#986 - «I envision myself achieving success in the workplace on a daily basis.»

#987 - «I am calm and centered within myself.»

#988 - «I treat all women with kindness, support, and encouragement.»

#989 - «Today, I will face every situation with grace and confidence.»

#990 - «I embrace my anxiety and all that it brings, knowing that it is a part of me.»

#991 - «I am filled with boundless love and positive energy, which radiate from within me.»

#992 - «I have the potential to achieve my aspirations and ambitions.»

#993 - «Every day presents an opportunity for growth and self-improvement.»

#994 - «I have faith in my capabilities to handle any obstacles that come my way.»

#995 - «My diligence and devotion will ultimately reap rewards.»

#996 - «I am deserving of love and admiration from those around me.»

#997 - «My focus is on the optimistic aspects of my life.»

#998 - «I have command over my emotions and thoughts.»

#999 - «I have trust in my ability to make sound judgments.»

#1000 - «I am encircled by loving and encouraging individuals.»

#1001 - «I am a powerful and capable person.»

#1002 - «I merit happiness and success.»

#1003 - «I am dedicated to my personal growth and development.»

#1004 - «I am capable of surmounting any barriers that present themselves.»

#1005 - «I appreciate the lessons learned through overcoming challenges.»

#1006 - «I am worthy of accomplishing my objectives and goals.»

#1007 - «I choose to relinquish pessimistic thoughts and attitudes.»

#1008 - «I have confidence in my capacity to manage any situation.»

#1009 - «I can construct the life that I aspire to live.»

#1010 - «I choose to be present and savor each moment.»

#1011 - «I have confidence in my intuition and inner wisdom.»

#1012 - «I am continuously improving, and thats perfectly acceptable.»

#1013 - «I appreciate my strengths and limitations.»

#1014 - «I merit love, respect, and kindness.»

#1015 - «I am capable of finding balance in my life.»

#1016 - «I am committed to living a purposeful and meaningful life.»

#1017 - «I am grateful for the struggles that have made me stronger.»

#1018 - «I am capable of learning from my errors and maturing.»

#1019 - «I deserve success and prosperity in all areas of my life.»

#1020 - «I choose to have faith in myself and my abilities.»

#1021 - «I am grateful for opportunities to learn and expand my knowledge.»

#1022 - «I can achieve my goals through patience and perseverance.»

#1023 - «I merit love and happiness and choose to cultivate it within myself.»

#1024 - «I trust the journey of my life and the path that it takes me on.»

#1025 - «I can create the life I want, one step at a time.»

#1026 - «I merit respect and acceptance for who I am.»

#1027 - «I am committed to prioritizing my well-being and self-care.»

#1028 - «I choose to forgive myself and others, letting go of past hurts.»

#1029 - «I am grateful for the abundance and wealth that surrounds me.»

#1030 - «I am capable of succeeding in the face of obstacles.»

#1031 - «I merit success in all aspects of my life, including my career, relationships, and personal growth.»

#1032 - «I trust my inner guidance and wisdom.»

#1033 - «I am grateful for the supportive and encouraging people in my life.»

#1034 - «I can make positive changes in my life and the world around me.»

#1035 - «I deserve a life filled with joy and fulfillment.»

#1036 - «I choose to focus on the positive in my life and appreciate what I have.»

#1037 - «I am committed to living a life aligned with my values and purpose.»

#1038 - «I am a resilient and strong woman.»

#1039 - «I trust my intuition and inner guidance.»

#1040 - «I choose to surround myself with positive and supportive people.»

#1041 - «I am confident in my ability to overcome obstacles.»

#1042 - «I am deserving of taking care of myself and loving myself»

#1043 - «I am empowered to make a positive impact on the world»

#1044 - «I embrace my unique qualities and celebrate my individuality»

#1045 - «I am worthy of abundance and success in all areas of my life»

#1046 - «I have the ability to make a difference in the lives of others»

#1047 - «I deserve happiness and fulfillment in my life»

#1048 - «I can overcome any obstacle with determination and resilience»

#1049 - «I am committed to prioritizing my physical, mental, and emotional well-being»

#1050 - «I deserve love and kindness, both from myself and others»

#1051 - «I trust in my own inner beauty and worthiness»

#1052 - «I am grateful for the support and love of the women in my life who inspire me»

#1053 - «I am confident in my own abilities and talents»

#1054 - «I am deserving of achieving my dreams and aspirations»

#1055 - «I embrace and honor my feminine power and energy»

#1056 - «I am capable of creating positive change in my community and beyond»

#1057 - «I deserve respect and equality in all areas of my life»

#1058 - «I trust in the power of my own voice and ideas to make a difference»

#1059 - «I am thankful for the opportunities that have allowed me to learn and grow»

#1060 - «I have the power to make a positive impact on the world»

#1061 - «I am deserving of success and recognition for my hard work and dedication»

#1062 - «I choose to let go of self-doubt and embrace my confidence and self-assurance»

#1063 - «I am confident in my ability to handle challenges with grace and resilience»

#1064 - «I am grateful for the trailblazing women who have come before me and paved the way»

#1065 - «I deserve equal opportunities and respect as men»

#1066 - «I trust in the power of sisterhood and the support of other women»

#1067 - «I am committed to living my life with authenticity and staying true to myself»

#1068 - «I have the potential to achieve greatness in my life»

#1069 - «I am worthy of admiration and respect from others»

#1070 - «I trust in my own abilities and skills to help me succeed»

## Embrace Positive Thinking: Concluding Thoughts on 1070 Daily Affirmations

Congratulations on completing "1070 Daily Affirmations: Transform Your Life with Positive Thinking!" I hope that this book has been a valuable tool in your journey towards personal growth and happiness. Remember, the power to transform your life lies within you, and by consistently practicing positive thinking and self-affirmation, you can achieve anything you set your mind to.

In this book, you have learned about the science behind affirmations, the benefits of daily affirmations, and you have been introduced to 1070 affirmations covering a wide range of topics. These affirmations were carefully crafted to help you overcome negative beliefs and attitudes, and to help you create positive habits and mindsets that will lead to a happier, more fulfilling life.

As you move forward, I encourage you to continue practicing positive thinking and self-affirmation daily. Make it a habit to repeat your favorite affirmations to yourself every morning and every night. You can also incorporate them into your daily routine by writing them down, reciting them during your daily commute, or even posting them on your mirror or computer screen.

Remember, positive thinking and self-affirmation are not a one-time fix. They are a lifelong practice that requires commitment and dedication. But with time and consistency, you will begin to see the positive changes in your life that you desire.

Thank you for choosing to embark on this journey with me. I wish you all the best in your personal and professional endeavors, and I hope that you continue to live your life with positivity, joy, and purpose.

Printed in Great Britain
by Amazon

28202733R00059